BANGKOK
ONLY YESTERDAY

STEVE VAN BEEK

Concept: Dean Barrett
Text: Steve van Beek
Design: Werner Hahn
Tony Chiu

Published by Hong Kong Publishing Company, Ltd.,
and in Thailand by Asia Book Company.

Designed by Grapho Ltd.
Printed in Hong Kong by Toppan (HK) Ltd.
ISBN: 962-7035-07-6

BANGKOK
ONLY YESTERDAY

STEVE VAN BEEK

Acknowledgements:

Grateful acknowledgement is given to Nid H. Shiranan, M.C. Piya Rangsit, M.L. Sumet Jumsai, Therd Suprichakorn and Kamolwan Sonsomsook for the help they gave in making this book possible.

The beginnings weren't all that promising. Bangkok's earliest inhabitants wore scales, fins and gills and weren't particularly interested in architecture, and even less in progress. In truth, 1,500 years ago, Bangkok lay beneath the ocean, a fact of birth it recalls in an annual return to the womb as it sinks beneath a slurry of floodwaters for two months.

Gradually, however, the annual pushing contest between the Chao Phya River transporting rich alluvial sediments to the sea and the incoming tides attempting to repulse its add-mirer, was won by the river. Like the lungfish forsaking their watery existence amid the primordial mangrove swamps, a town, like Atlantis in reverse, began to emerge from the sea.

Even a few centuries ago, there was little to indicate the tiny community had any future. Maps referred to the area as "Talay Tom" or the "Sea of Mud". Primitive thatched houses stood high on stilts on land hard-won by digging channels and heaping the earth to create islands for yards and gardens. It was a technique that later would be the rationale for creating lakes in the city's parks and palaces and which today is the principal form of agricultural tillage in the truck gardens and coconut plantations of Thonburi to the west.

The channels between the islands became waterways. Skimmed by tiny banana-shaped wooden boats, the watery maze threading its way through the silted archipelago formed the sole means of communication and transportation.

The creation of Bangkok as an entity was accomplished by shovel blade. Seeking to cut travel time between the sea and his capital at Ayutthaya, King Phrajai (1534-1546) set teams of corvee laborers to work digging a two-kilometer channel across the neck of a 17-kilometer loop of the river. The river, the sculptor and moulder of the city, gently nibbled at the canal's banks, widening them to become its main course and reducing the former loop to the Bangkok Noi and Bangkok Yai canals.

The entrance to the Bangkok Yai canal marked the farthest point north that deep-draft ships could travel. There, they furled their sails and transferred their cargoes to lighters for the remaining 88 km journey to Ayutthaya, Thailand's capital from 1350 to 1767. It was inevitable that a town would grow up to serve the sea-weary sailors and provide the small boats for upriver transshipment.

Joost Schouten, Director of the East India Company in 1636 noted that ships "...enter the River without any more danger of running on ground till they come to the Town of Banckock, six Dutch miles upwards; then the River grows narrower and more shallow. Ships drawing eleven or twelve foot water being scarce able to mount to the City of India (Ayutthaya) where they are sometimes forced to stay till the moneths of September, October and November for water to return. The Country is generally well peopled, especially the lower part of it, being full of Villages and Towns."

Later travelers noted the richness of the land and the huge fruit orchards that covered it. The settlement on the left bank was established as a Customs port and soon gained great prosperity as evidenced by the name given it: Thonburi ("money town").

Its strategic location at the gateway to the country led King Narai (1657-1688) to build a fortress amid the wild olive or plum trees (the actual fruit "kok" not existing in the English gardener's lexicon) of Bangkok to control traffic up and down the river. He engaged a team of French engineers to construct a star-shaped bastion 300 m × 300 m that ran from Rajinee School to the Grand Palace or roughly opposite the mouth of Bangkok Yai Canal.

The fortress had a very short life because a few kilometers upstream, the French engineers' monkish brothers were meddling in Thai politics in the hopes of converting the entire country to Christianity. Their grand scheme unravelled with the

A 17th century map of the lower part of the Chao Phya River showing Bangkok occupying both sides of the river. In the last quarter of the 17th century hundreds of French soldiers and several French priests arrived in Siam and made their way upriver to Ayudhya, written on the map as "Ville de Siam."
(Steve Van Beek)

5

death of King Narai in 1688. The victor in the struggle for the throne, King Petchraja, led a faction that had been smouldering for some time over the foreigners' usurption of power and when they got their chance, resorted to armed force to throw them out of the country.

The French retreated to Bangkok and holed up in the fortress they had just built. The excellence of the engineers' craftsmanship was proven by the inability of a large Thai army to dislodge them. After several months, everyone decided they had had enough and the French boarded their ships and sailed away.

King Petchraja had had a large dose of proof of what could happen if such a strategic building fell into the wrong hands and ordered it partially dismantled. The remainder was torn down by King Rama I in 1782 to make room for his palace.

The next people to flee Ayutthaya and find refuge in Bangkok were the Thais themselves. In 1767, the Burmese armies succeeded in their centuries-long struggle to break the back of the Thai empire. Their exultation led to the absolute destruction of Ayutthaya, reducing its population from one million to little more than 10,000.

With remnants of the Thai army, a recalcitrant Chinese-Thai general named Taksin routed the Burmese occupiers. Deciding Ayutthaya was too difficult to defend, he moved to Thonburi. Over the next decade, he was so busy fighting the Burmese that he had little time to build a palace but lived in the mansion of the former governor behind crenelated walls near the present Temple of Dawn. He did see the strategic advantages of Bangkok, however, and in the little spare time he had available he had Klong (canal) Lawd dug to create an island at the point where the peninsula of Bangkok was wreathed by the river on three sides. On the inner bank of the canal, he built a defensive wall and there are many indications that he intended to move a large part of his capital into Bangkok.

Both sides of the river had been developing at an equal pace. The Chinese who made their fortunes in Thonburi had built their homes and set up businesses just north of the walls of the original Bangkok fortress. Numerous temples like Wat Po, Wat Saket, Wat Samplum and Wat Sampeng served as the nuclei for small communities whose borders soon began to merge with those of their neighbors. The tiny village of Bangkok was beginning to push aside the wild plum/olive trees and emerge as a metropolis.

King Taksin's successor, King Rama I, was a dreamer with a sense of grandeur. He recognized that his people were exhausted after decades of fighting the Burmese and that they needed some visible assertion of their former greatness to inspire them. In his design for the future, Rama I was thinking of dynasty rather than life kingship and wanted his own tangible reminder of the potency of his and his descendents' rule.

His model was Ayutthaya, the famed "City of Angels" whose memory still stirred his subjects' hearts. Ayuttaya had been an island and it was necessary to create an island for his new capital bigger than the one Taksin had made. Thonburi lacked an area with the proper configurations but the Bangkok side, though lower and subject to floods, was peninsular and thus ideally suited to his purposes.

The site where he wished to build his palace was occupied by Chinese merchants. He asked them to move to an area to the east which became known as Sampheng, the future Chinatown. He then began his work in earnest.

With a keen awareness of the weight of symbology, he concentrated the three pillars of the country — the monarchy, religion and national administration — within the same grounds.

His initial task was to decree the existence of the city proper. On April 21, 1782, 54 minutes after the first rays of dawn crested the horizon, he erected Lak Muang, the city pillar, a scant 15 days after declaring the establishment of the Chakri dynasty and the foundation of a new capital. He then set off on a giant building scheme involving the Grand Palace, Wat Phra Kaew and other major temples, a task which would take 20 years.

The first seat of national power was a mother-of-pearl inlaid teak throne. It sat in a wooden house surrounded by a wooden palisade which served until 1785 when a permanent palace was completed. His delay in building a palace was because his main priority was to construct a home for the tiny jasper image that for most Thais symbolized the essence of Buddhism: the Emerald Buddha.

His intention that his capital be a holy city rather than simply a seat of secular power is indicated by one of the names he gave his island-city, Rattanakosin, meaning "Resting Place of the Emerald Buddha".

As much to create an emotional link with the former capital as to obtain building materials, he despatched convoys of corvee laborers and war captives to Ayutthaya. They dismantled the ruined buildings and transported the bricks by fleets of barges to the landing at Tha Chang next to the palace. For three years, thousands of workers, like an ant army walked gangplanks beneath their brick burdens which were used to build thick defensive walls around the palace and the city.

To extend the boundaries of the city, Rama I ordered that a new canal be dug in a concentric arc farther to the east. More than 10,000 Cambodian captives were pressed into service to dig Banglampoo Canal (so named for the "lampoo" trees that lined it) and its extension to the south, Ong Ang Canal (for the many "ong" or water jars found in the area).

An additional 5,000 Laotian captives were brought from Vientiane to erect high crenelated walls around the entire city with 14 octagonal watchtowers built every 400 meters. With the thick walls and the surrounding moat, the island-city, roughly the shape of a sacred conch shell, was virtually impregnable. Reluctant to allow future enemies access to the city, he built only one bridge, this after much debate, and it was a revolving bridge that could be swung aside to prevent the enemy's crossing it.

In this very serious endeavor, there was one touch of whimsy. Rama I ordered that Klong Mahanak be dug running east from Klong Banglampoo past what would one day be the Golden Mount. The Dynastic Chronicles record that "He wanted it to be a place where the people of the capital city could go boating and singing and reciting poems during the high-water season just like the custom observed in the former capital of Ayutthaya."

Late in 1784, the finial was placed on Wat Phra Kaew, the Temple of the Emerald Buddha, and the time for the installation of the image was at hand. Early in the morning, throngs gathered on the riverbanks and along the roads to watch as the small Emerald Buddha was taken out of the Thonburi palace and carried to the river's edge. There, it was placed on a golden royal barge rowed by red-jacketed oarsmen who chanted solemnly in a deep bass tone as they dipped flashing paddles in the broad Chao Phya River and pulled the great barge to the Bangkok side. On arrival, the tiny image was reverently carried in a splendid procession to the new temple and, amid the chanting of tiers of orange-robed monks who lined either side of the great hall and amid fragrant tendrils of incense smoke carrying their prayers heavenwards, it was placed in its permanent home high above the prostrated worshippers, the king prominent among them.

In the 15th century, the Thai armies had completed the destruction of the Khmer empire. Part of their war booty were the Brahmin priests who had conducted the Khmer court ceremonies using rituals brought from India centuries before. The Thais had found the Brahmins' rites particularly appealing and had installed the priests in the Ayutthayan courts where they decreed court procedure and etiquette. It was felt that the Brahmins needed a temple of their own. Rama I was also eager to erect a second huge temple at what was then considered to be the center of the royal city.

Accordingly, in 1784, the massive Wat Suthat was built and nearby it the Brahmin temple was constructed. In front of Wat Suthat, a 21.15 meter Giant Swing was raised as the central stage for the annual 10-day ceremony honoring the god Isuan's (Shiva) visit to earth. A noisy festival with almost continuous dramatic performances and myriad stalls selling foods and sweets was capped by a contest in which quartets of swarthy young men would climb atop a wide board suspended by thick ropes from the Giant Swing's crosspiece. They would begin the rhythmic straining that would turn the board into a giant pendulum, swinging back and forth, gradually climbing higher and higher until they reached an altitude 15 meters above the ground where one would attempt to snatch a bag of gold hung on a tall pole. It was not unusual for a contestant to misjudge and find himself free-falling to his death.

So important was the area that one of the city's three roads, Thanon Sao Chinacha (Giant Swing Road), later renamed Bamrungmuang, led straight to it from the palace wall. A second road circled the palace and a third traced the inner side of the city wall. Beyond the walls, a few dusty tracks plodded by lumbering elephants led through the commoners' settlements and to the jungles beyond. For the most part, however, transport was still by the canals which crisscrossed the fruit plantations and rice fields.

In 1785, with many of the buildings in the city completed, the king commanded that a grand celebration be held. Buddhist monks were invited to chant mantras on the city walls with one monk sitting in each battlement. Royal funds were used to buy rice and condiments for offerings to the monks and meal stations were set up at various points around the city to feed the populace, compliments of the king. Coins were also tossed to the crowds for a period of three days. Theaters were erected along the streets and performances were given round the clock.

Daily life in the city began with the striking of a huge drum named Phra Surasai in the three-tier drumtower southeast of the palace. The deep boom each dawn reverberated across the rooftops and signalled the guards to open the city's huge gates thus marking the commencement of daily commerce. Vendors entered the city to congregate at the markets to sell fresh produce brought to the gates on sampans in the pre-dawn hours. Commoners employed by the palace would begin the long trudge to their official duties.

The king began his day by walking to the throne hall where he served food to a gathering of Buddhist monks. After listening to treasury reports about the disbursement of monies, he would go to the royal audience hall to hear judicial cases and reports on the progress of governmental affairs. Following this, he would go to the Inner Court to discuss palace affairs before retiring to his own quarters.

The end of the day was marked by the same resonant boom of the drum struck at sunset to signal the closing of the palace gates. Commoners from outlying areas would rest for the night in special pavilions erected just outside the gates as the city's earliest hotels.

Within the palace, the king would have his evening meal and then listen to a Buddhist sermon. After holding audience with his principal courtiers and hearing medical reports on those of the royal family or entourage who had been ill, he would assign royal pages to check the progress of construction projects and deliver their reports the following evening. Following a final general audience lasting until 9 or 10 p.m., he would retire for the night.

The drumtower also held a middle-sized and small-sized drum. On the tier above the giant Phra Surasai drum was the Aka nee Pii Nag which was beat three times if there was a fire beyond the city walls and was beat continuously until any fire within the walls was extinguished. The topmost drum, the tiny Phikaad Phairee, was struck if an enemy was sighted approaching the city.

The three drums served as the city's communications network until the 1860s

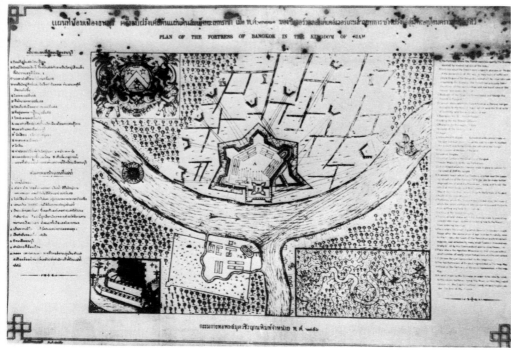

when Rama IV decided they were unfashionable and the mark of a backward country. He had the drumtower torn down and installed cannons on the corners of the palace wall to act as the city's alarm system, a custom borrowed from Singapore. There are no reports on how the populace reacted to the rude insistence of a cannon boom at dawn.

In 1789, extensive repairs began on Photharam Temple, an undertaking that lasted 12 years. When finished, the temple was renamed Wat Chetuporn but continued to be known popularly as Wat Po. Numerous other temples were restored or built anew, a sign that the kingdom was beginning to regain some of the prosperity formerly enjoyed by Ayutthaya. The same year, the Royal Chronicles, the official records of the period, note that lightning struck the Amarintharaphisek royal Audience Hall and caused a big fire. Among the firefighters was the king who personally toted out the heavy teak throne to save it from the flames.

Among the otherwise pedestrian entries in the Royal Chronicles for 1788 is a droll account of a pair of French brothers who stepped off their ship one day and announced that one was a professional boxer and the other his manager and that they were ready to take on all comers for a wager. The Chronicles note that the king was informed of the challenge and consulted his younger brother, the heir apparent, on what they should do. The brother, somewhat of a hothead, advised that "If we don't send someone to fight a match with these white men, they who are foreigners would look down on us and say that this country has no boxer at all good enough to fight them. This would blemish the honor of Your Majesty in all countries. I will take it upon myself to find a good boxer to fight the white men and to bring us victory."

The stakes were set and a rude boxing ring built near the theater. The Thai boxer, a stocky young man named Mun Phlan, was covered in magical herbal oils to make him invulnerable. At the bell, the Frenchman charged out of his corner.

"The white man reached out to seize Mun Phlan and break his collarbone. Mun Phlan raised up his arms to prevent that and struck out at the white man while moving backwards. The white man was hit but did not fall and kept reaching for Mun Phlan who in turn kept stepping backwards while hitting. Thus, the white man could not get at and seize him.

"The white man's elder brother saw this, leaped up, went over and pushed Mun Phlan so he could not backstep any farther and avoid his opponent...The

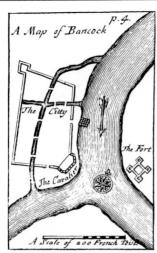

A map of Bangkok in the year 1687 sketched by La Loubere, a French cleric and one of the leaders of a French embassy to Siam. It was during this period that the Greek adventurer, Constantine Phaulkon, rose to great power as "Lord of Victory" under the Siamese monarch, Narai the Great.
(Steve Van Beek)

king's younger brother...became angry and asked why then the other should help, making it two on the other side. The prince quickly jumped off the platform, brought his foot up and kicked the elder white man who tumbled down. The referees there rushed in and began fighting with the two white brothers. Both brothers were badly hurt. Their subordinates then carried them back to their ship. The king ordered that government medicine doctors and masseurs go to their ship to treat them."

Rama I's younger brother figures in another bizarre incident that nearly spelled the end of the newly-founded kingdom in 1796. A big boat race had been planned pitting the team of the king and his brother against each other. Prior to the race, the two teams were sized up to ensure they were equal in weight and height. The brother, however, secretly substituted a bigger set of oarsmen for the race. When the king learned of the deceit, he cancelled the race making his brother lose a great deal of face.

Two months later, the brother appeared at a royal audience to demand extra funds to pay his retainers. Rama I told him this was impossible because that year's revenues had not been collected. The brother stormed off in a fury demanding revenge.

The brother occupied the Palace of the Front (Wang Na) which today incorporates the National Museum. Until Rama V dismantled it, the wall of Wang Na emcompassed the northern half of Sanam Luang, an area that was used as a drill ground for the heir apparent's soldiers.

When the prince returned to his palace still very angry, he ordered that guards be posted along the walls and that all the cannon be aimed at the Grand Palace. On learning of his brother's intentions, the alarmed king ordered that his cannons be turned on the Wang Na. It looked as though the work of the past 15 years was about to be blown away when the pair's elder sisters rushed to the scene and implored the brothers to remember all they had been through together. Chagrined, the heir apparent went to ask forgiveness of his elder brother and from that day hence, there was peace between them.

Sanam Luang, the wide, grassy esplanade separating the Grand Palace and the Palace of the Front had a number of functions as the years passed. Its principal purpose was as a cremation ground for royal funerals. Huge ornate pavilions would be erected specially for the funerals and dismantled once the body had been consumed on the funeral pyre. The pavilions became more and more elaborate to the point that at the end of the 18th century, it was decided to build a special permanent building at the western side of the ground for funeral ceremonies. After it was completed, it was felt that it would be unfitting to have a building with such a macabre purpose and with ghosts flitting around it so it was made into the National Library and later the Fine Arts Department which it houses today.

During the 1830s when the country was threatened by Vietnamese armies poised to pour across the border, Rama III (1824-1851) ordered that the Sanam Luang be sown in rice seed. When the Vietnamese envoys arrived to declare war, they were astounded to see that the Thais were growing food right in the middle of the city so that in the event of a seige they could hold out indefinitely. The shaken envoys returned to their generals to report that it would be folly to attack such a well-provisioned city. The generals listened and then withdrew their armies and Thailand was spared an invasion.

It was to combat the Vietnamese threat that King Rama III extended the Mahanak Canal to Chachoengsao for the purpose of moving troops quickly from the city into the war zone. For years, the waterway was the sole means of penetrating the countryside to the east.

By the mid-1800s, the city was beginning to mushroom outward to the north, east and south. Distinct ethnic districts emerged comprised of refugees from neighboring countries or of families who had arrived in Bangkok as captives. Within the city wall was Ban Tanao comprised of Mons who had come from Tenasserim, Burma. In the area of Pan Fah Bridge at the site of the Thai Niyom Building was a palace inhabited by Khmer royalty. As a result, the area running through Ban Dokmai and Ban Baat became known as Ban Kamain (Village of Cambodians). To the north in the Samsen area was Ban Yuan (Vietnamese) and to the southwest was Ban Tawai, named for the Burmese timber merchants originally from Tavoy, Burma. Farther east was Makassan inhabited by Muslims who had arrived from Makassar, Indonesia.

At the same time, streets and sections associated with particular trades grew up. Thanon Ti Thong (Beat Gold Street) near Wat Suthat reverberated with the thump of brass hammers reducing gold ingots to flat sheets to be applied to Buddha images to make merit. Ban Baat (Monk's Bowl Village), Ban Bu (bronze bowls), Bang Chang Lor (iron workers), Ban Kamin (cumin powder), Thanon Din Sor (chalk), Ban Maw (rice cooking pots and other types of pottery) and Ban Dok Mai (fireworks) described the trades carried out by their inhabitants. No one has yet discovered the trade carried out in Bang Rak (love) district.

In the 1830s, a new landmark changed the city's skyline. As in Bangkok, a canal named Klong Mahanak had flowed through Ayutthaya. Beside it had been a Phu Kho Thong or Golden Mount and Rama III decided he wanted to recreate one by Bangkok's mahanak canal and next to Wat Saket. The Ayutthayan Golden Mount had been hardly more than a hillock and Rama III didn't feel it rated the appellation of mountain. What he wanted was a real mountain.

Thick timber and laterite was used for the base but the weight proved too much for the soft ground and it burst while the second tier was being constructed, dashing Rama III's hopes.

The work was abandoned until Rama IV (1851-1868) who resumed the project but was also defeated by soft earth. It was only after 1,000 stout logs were sunk as pilings that the 80-meter-tall mountain was completed and a golden chedi placed atop it in 1863. In 1877, ashes of the Buddha were placed in the chedi.

The mountain was a unique addition to the city, an assertion that Bangkok had risen above the primordial muck, its tree-clad slopes thrusting into the sky. It offered a panoramic view of the city, a place to appreciate what Bangkok had achieved in the space of a few years. From it, one could look at the moat and the crenelated walls that surrounded the royal city, beyond to the Giant Swing and, tracing the dusty path west, to the knobbed walls that surrounded the shimmering Emerald Buddha complex and the Grand Palace. Farther on was the broad silvery band of the Chao Phya River and the newly-erected Wat Arun, the Temple of Dawn, sitting on the dusk side of the river.

In between and outside the walls were trees, trees and more trees causing early foreign visitors to remark on the city's garden-like setting, the brilliant green of the trees hanging over the quiet canals lined by small teak houses with vegetable gardens separating them.

The Golden Mount's value as a vantage point was not lost on Chao Phya Surasakmontri, chief counsellor to Rama V (1868-1910) who wanted to turn it into a Gibraltar of the East. Noting that it enjoyed a broad view of the river and of ships running up and down it, he suggested to Rama V that the chedi be torn down and that the hilltop bristle with cannons capable of blasting ships out of the waters beyond the Grand Palace. Given the inaccuracy of the day's ordnance, it was just as likely that the cannon balls would have fallen short and destroyed the city, a prospect Rama V recognized at once.

He agreed instead to a proposal that watchmen be armed with flags and stationed atop the mountain to signal the approach of the enemy. They led an easy life as never until World War II was the city threatened and at that point, sirens were felt to be a more noticeable method of raising the alarm when bombers approached. By that time, however, the Golden Mount had been shorn of much of its beauty. In 1929, its trees were chopped down and its slopes were sealed in cement, perhaps prophetic of the fate that would befall the rest of the city in the succeeding decades.

At the base of the Golden Mount was Wat Saket which played a rather grisly role in the early days of the city: that of a charnelhouse in times of plague. While royal cremations were carried out at Sanam Luang, the bodies of commoners were carried through the Pratu Phi (Ghost Gate) at the end of Sao Ching Cha Road and to one of the surrounding temples, Wat Saket being the most popular.

When plague struck the city, however, there were too many bodies to burn and they were left in the open courtyard. Soon the sky above the city would turn black as thousands of vultures soared over it trying to trace the odor of carrion. They would then alight to fight with the pyre dogs to strip the bodies of their flesh. In the reign of Rama II (1809-1824), an epidemic had killed 30,000 people and the roads to the temples were filled with a constant procession of litters borne by weeping relatives on the way to dispose of their dead. Plague struck the city in nearly regular 10-year cycles in 1873, 1881, 1891 and 1900 killing 10,000 each time until sanitation was improved.

The vultures also descended whenever an execution took place. Royal murderers had their titled heads removed at Wat Patoomkongka at the eastern end of Sampeng Lane while commoners were executed at Wat Makassan east of Pratunam. Their bodies met the same fate; to be laid out as a feast for the vultures.

As well as growing upward, the city was growing outward. Foreigners who had been barred from the country after the intrigues of 1688 had made their peace with the throne and by 1850 the area in the vicinity of the Oriental Hotel was covered in European-style houses, embassies, legations, hotels and stores selling imported goods. Cargoes made their way to the inner city from the docks along the labyrinthine network of canals that by now crisscrossed the city or along the few elephant tracks that meandered among the wooden houses and buildings.

By 1855, however, the city had grown to 300,000 people and a quicker, more efficient network for travel was required. Thus, when the foreigners petitioned King Rama IV to build roads where they could drive horses and carriages to take the evening air, they found a ready response.

Rama IV was acutely aware of his capital's deficiencies and was seeking ways to modernize it. A royal edict in 1857 commanded that a 6.5 kilometer road be constructed from the city gate along the river to the point where the river turned east. At the same time, he ordered the metalling of the old Sao China Cha Road leading to the Giant Swing and the gate beyond and decreed the construction of a third road to link the two.

An indication of the high hopes he held for the roads' contributions to the city's progress can be found in the names he gave each of them. Charoen Krung, best known to foreigners as New Road, meant "city progress or prosperity"; Bamrung-muang translated as "growth" and Fuang Nakorn, the link road, meant "to bring fame".

The design of New Road caused some controversy among the city planners. The original idea was to build it straight east from the city gate but military strategists feared it would give a direct line shot to enemy cannoners camped in front of it. They therefore designed a kink in it so as it left the gate and crossed the Ong Ang canal/moat, it angled off to the right. In 1862, King Rama IV completed the road by ordering construction of a further 900-meter link between Wat Po and the city gate at a cost of 19,700 baht. He also ordered that shops be built along it and rented to merchants.

Soon after, the king was complaining that only half the road was being used and that the other half was covered in grass and beginning to deteriorate. Growing traffic soon took care of that so that by 1890, complaints were being heard that with all the carriages the road was too narrow. The lovely trees that had lined it were cut, sewers and sidewalks were installed and a once-beautiful section of the city was transformed.

From the main spine of Charoen Krung, new roads spread out in either direction. Most prominent were Si Phya (Four Generals), Silom (Windmill) and Sathorn. The names of several of the smaller lanes along the southern section of New Road were Thai transliterations of the names of foreigners who lived or worked on them. Thus, today one can still see Kaptan Bush Lane, Maw Smit Street (Dr. Smith), Rong Luey Misglug Lane (Klugg's Sawmill) and Rong Luey Asiatic Lane (East Asiatic Sawmill).

By 1880, big changes were transforming the once-quiet capital of the Chakri kings. Under the guidance of reform-minded King Chulalongkorn (Rama V), new machinery was being introduced to make life easier and more comfortable. In 1884, a court official turned a switch and the Grand Palace glowed with electric lights. By 1897, electricity was being supplied to the entire city.

Horse-drawn trams were introduced in 1888. Approximately 800 ponies pulled carriages with first and second-class compartments along twin rails running beside the Grand Palace and down New Road with feeder lines branching off at major intersections. On Feb. 1, 1893, Bangkok became the first city in the East to have electric trams. They were installed by a team of Danish engineers 10 years before Copenhagen had a similar system. By 1901, the tram network extended more than 20 km operating more than 2,800 car/miles per day as far south as Paknam.

The trams were key participants in a drama that was played out on the Chinatown section of New Road one day in 1889. Chinatown had always been one of the city's more colorful sections with a cast of unique characters running various licit and illicit activities.

One of the most powerful was a gangster named Ang Yi. In 1889, his gang split into two factions and a major battle for control of the New Road area was soon under way.

On June 19, residents along New Road began scurrying for cover as the two gangs tore zinc sheets from fences and hauled furniture out of houses to build barricades across the street. Using clubs, knives and guns, hundreds of gangsters began a battle that lasted all night leaving 20 dead and at least 100 injured when dawn broke the following day. Even then, the dispute was far from resolved.

A police force comprised of 55 Malays and Indians had been formed in 1862. By 1889 it had grown to nearly 1,200 men the majority of them Thais. But they couldn't muster the gunpower to rout the gangsters so they called in the army.

On June 21, two days into the battle, the officers put their heads together and decided the only solution was to move quickly and catch the gangs by surprise while they were regrouping their forces. They chose the trams as their transport and, bells clanging furiously, bore down New Road in several cars, guns blazing, which prompted both gangs to open fire on them. The battle lasted five hours but when the smoke cleared, 10 gangsters had been killed, 20 wounded and 800 arrested including eight of Ang Yi's top brass. New Road hasn't been that exciting since.

Chinatown at the end of the century had a reputation for hot times. It was constantly threatened by fire which would sweep through the narrow alleyways or leap from roof to overlapping roof. Because of this, many houses had shallow wells beneath. When there was a fire all the valuables would be thrown into this and sealed over. After one disastrous fire in 1900, Rama V banned thatched roofs and personally drew up plans for Songwat Road to allow better access into the area.

Sampheng was also the city's red light district, or in local parlance, the "green light" district for the green lanterns which hung above the brothel doors. The girls who lived there were referred to politely as "Ying Kom Khiew" or "green lantern women" who commanded fees of one baht a night.

Most of the brothels with Thai and Chinese women were in Trok Tao where famed madams, Mae Fang, Mae Kleep and Mae Tao, had their establishments. Mae Fang made so much money that to atone for her life of sin, she used her earnings to build a temple called "Wat Mae Yai Fang" or Madam Fang's temple, later renamed Wat Kanikaphol but still known to local residents by her name.

At the mouth of Trok Tao, Mae Kleep also built a temple called Wat Kanmathyaram after her son who later became a famous Buddhist monk named Phra Darunraksa. Higher-class establishments were located in big hotels on Siphya and Surawongse Roads and were staffed by Japanese and European women who charged four baht a night.

King Rama V began a land rush when he built his new palace at Dusit Park. In 1902, Rajdamnern Road was built by royal proclamation and the city's better families began to build mansions in the area. He also had Wat Benchamabopit, the Marble Temple, built, the last major temple construction to take place in Bangkok. More streets were built and by 1908, some 300 cars were popping and putting along the thoroughfares, the king's yellow electric car prominent among them.

By 1912, Bangkok had a population of 630,000 or approximately one-ninth of the population of Thailand. While the city was growing it was beginning to deal with some of the problems that had, literally, been plaguing it.

Rev. Bradley in his "Bangkok Diary" of 1836 had complained about people throwing trash under their houses or in the river. Rama IV in 1856 had decreed a prohibition against throwing dead animals into the klongs. Numerous edicts were issued and gradually they began to have some effect. By 1900, foreign residents were commenting that the city had become noticeably cleaner. One major step in the right direction came in 1903 with the creation of a freshwater system, though the first potable water didn't begin to flow until Nov. 14, 1914.

The air age came to Thailand in 1911 when a tiny French plane dropped out of the sky onto the Royal Bangkok Sport's Club field which had been part of Rama V's country retreat, the Srapratoom Palace, before he donated it to the club. By World War I, Thailand had its own air arm piloted by Thais.

A foreign visitor, W.A. Graham, provided a very clear picture of how much the city had changed when in a 1912 guidebook titled "Siam" he noted that "the streets are as a rule well paved and metalled and are kept fairly clean, those nearest to the Palace being in the best condition as being the more likely to catch the eye of Royalty. They are continually crowded with traffic of all kinds, thousands of jinrickshaws, hundreds of horsed carriages and motor vehicles continually passing to and fro.

"Here and there a row of the older thatched dwellings persists and a few floating houses still cling to the banks of the river and principal creeks but these are doomed to early extinction. The picturesque castellated fortifications of the city are going also, the gateways have nearly all been removed to facilitate traffic and whole sections of the walls have been demolished and utilised as road-metal.

"Before long, Bangkok will be a city of bricks but it will be also a city of trees, the verdure of which, together with the graceful spires and bright-coloured roofs of its religious and public buildings will always redeem it from the monotony of appearance which characterizes many cities of the West."

High hopes indeed but the changes he was seeing were continuing to alter the face of the city. Residents seeking respite were beginning to head for the suburbs or creating oases in enclaves in the city.

Escape from the closeness of the city was accomplished by railway. Sportsmen took the train to shoot snipe at Sala Ya on the Southern Line or north to Klong Rangsit. Most roads went no farther than the edge of the city. Erik Seidenfaden makes them seem particularly refreshing in his guidebook of 1927 where he says "in the immediate outskirts of the city are found excellent motoring roads lined with trees whose overhanging branches intertwine and effectually screen the passenger from the rays of the sun. These long, straight, shady avenues which have an appearance almost cloistral leave an unforgettable impression on the visitor. In no other city is it possible so often to turn from the throng of a city street and to find oneself miraculously, it would seem, in a little residential quarter of half a dozen bungalows,

each sitting cool and sequestered in a large compound that is tree-covered, green and refreshing."

Echoing Graham's optimistic hopes, he said "the future will see Bangkok as a vast well laid-out, park-like town intersected with a network of broad shady roads running in all directions...In the future when the road from Bangkok reaches Paknam this place will become another suburb of the capital as the new road will be quickly lined with houses and residences of people who seek to get away from the capital out to the cool breezes of the sea."

We know differently today for the road described was Sukhumvit, now a concrete canyon.

Bangkok reached back to its origins when the Phra Buddha Yot Fa Bridge (Memorial Bridge) was built to link the city with Thonburi. Opened with great fanfare on April 6, 1932, it was the centerpiece in a grand celebration to mark the 150th anniversary of the city's establishment as the country's capital and of the founding of the Chakri dynasty. At that time, the bridge dropped into virtual jungle but it was only a short while before Thonburi began to resemble Bangkok.

By 1960, nearly all the canals had been filled in to accommodate the heavy traffic of thousands of people rushing to somewhere else. Looking at it today, it is difficult to imagine that only yesterday, Bangkok was an idyllic city, the garden spot of the East where peace and tranquility reigned. It has retained much of its beauty but one has to plunge deep into the side lanes or into private gardens to recapture that beauty.

What remains as a shining reminder of the glory that the first Chakri kings envisioned for their capital is the Grand Palace and the beautiful Wat Phra Kaew, the principal buildings of the Rattanakosin Island. In this, its Bicentennial year, Bangkok is beginning to awaken to a memory of Rama I's vision and to recreate some of the splendor the city formerly boasted. Perhaps by 2082, Bangkok Only Yesterday will be what its first rulers envisioned it to be: the jewelled city of the East, an abode of angels created as an earthly paradise to be shared by angels and mortals alike.

An early sketch of Paknam where tall masted ships passed on their way to Bangkok. The sketch dates from around 1850.
(Chalie Iamkrasin)

17

A royal barge oarsman photographed about 1910. This was perhaps one of the most serene and beautiful periods of Bangkok's history.
(Steve Van Beek)

Left: New Road in the foreign section of town. The tall white building at the center is Whiteaway Laidlaw Co., the most famous department store. To the right out of sight was the British legation, now the site of the General Post Office. 1900.
(Therd Suprichakorn)

Center: New Road about 1920.
(Patricia Cheeseman)

Bottom: The British Club in 1915. It looks the same today.
(Therd Suprichakorn)

Elephant soldiers with "modern" guns in front of the palace wall about 1910.
(Steve Van Beek)

Elephants with the beautiful howdahs reserved for the use of royalty, photographed near the Grand Palace.
(Steve Van Beek)

Facing page: A quartet of contestants in the Giant Swing Contest. During incredibly daring swinging feats at the Giant Swing *(Sao Ching Cha)*, teams of men swung a full 180° arc. The Swinging Ceremony was held in honor of Phra Isuan, a Brahmin god. The ceremony was abolished in 1935.
(National Archives, Bangkok)

View from the Golden Mount looking southwest. Below are the monks' quarters at Wat Saket. The smokestack in the far distance is the electricity generating plant at Wat Lieb which produced Bangkok's first electricity in 1897. In the right part of the center panel can be seen the original iron trestle bridge that crossed Ong Ang Canal on its way down Bamrungmuang Road. In the right panel can be seen the city wall and beyond it Wat Suthat, the Giant Swing, Wat Arun to the left and Wat Phra Kaew to the right. 1900.
(M.C. Piya Rangsit)

23

Looking from the Royal Landing across to Wat Arun with the royal yacht, the *Maha Chakri*, moored midstream at right.
(M.C. Piya Rangsit)

The river front upstream from the Grand Palace. Both photographs show the beauty of the river about 1900.
(M.C. Piya Rangsit)

A grand floating procession near the Grand Palace in honor of King Rama V. The "Royal Barge" ceremony on Bangkok's Chao Phya river is one of Asia's most spectacular sights. The royal barges have remained much the same from the time of early European accounts written during the late 17th century.
(Steve Van Beek)

Two young princes ready for the ceremony of cutting of the topknots. This ceremony is performed on children approaching adolescence. According to Hindu tradition, the boy will have turned thirteen and a girl will have turned eleven. The ceremony involves Hindu traditions, Buddhist services, the entertainment of friends and relatives, a ritualistic ablution, and the elaborate dressing of the child. The ornate costume of princes often included sandals of gold brocade and a gold or diamond multi-tiered headdress for the topknot. (Steve Van Beek)

28

King Rama VI (King Vajiravudh) with his court. The photograph was taken about 1920.
(Steve Van Beek)

A young boy with his topknot. The actual moment for the cutting of the topknot was set by a Brahmin. The cost and ornateness of the child's dress was an indication of the social and financial position of his parents.
(Steve Van Beek)

Children of King Rama V (Chulalongkorn) with the first gramophone ever to arrive in Thailand. The photograph was taken about 1895.
(National Archives, Bangkok)

King Rama V's children with their cameras. The solemn lad second from right was Somdej Chaophya Mahidol Adulyadej Kromaluang Songklanakarin, the father of King Bhumibol, the kingdom's present ruler. The photograph was taken about 1910.
(National Archives, Bangkok)

View from Bangkok
looking across the Chao
Phra River to Wat Arun,
the Temple of Dawn.
Pieces of multicolored
Chinese porcelain are
embedded in the cement
of the great *prang*, or
rounded spire. The spire
rises 79 meters and is still
one of the tallest religious
structures in the country.
(M.C. Piya Rangsit)

Chao Chun Uab, one of King Rama V's favorite wives. The photograph was taken about 1905.
(Chalie Iamkrasin)

A young girl with her topknot. If the child's parents were financially well off, Buddhist and Brahminical services would be followed by an elaborate dinner and open-air theatrical performances.
(National Archives, Bangkok)

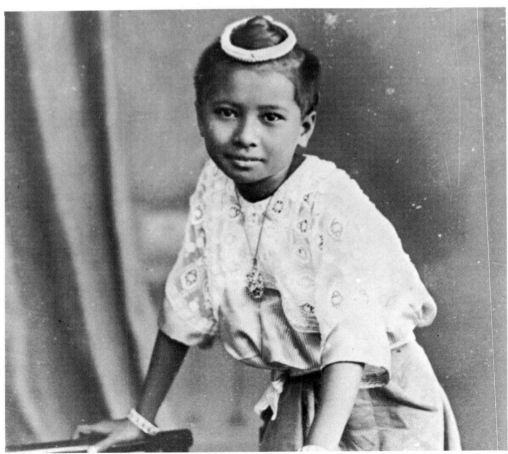

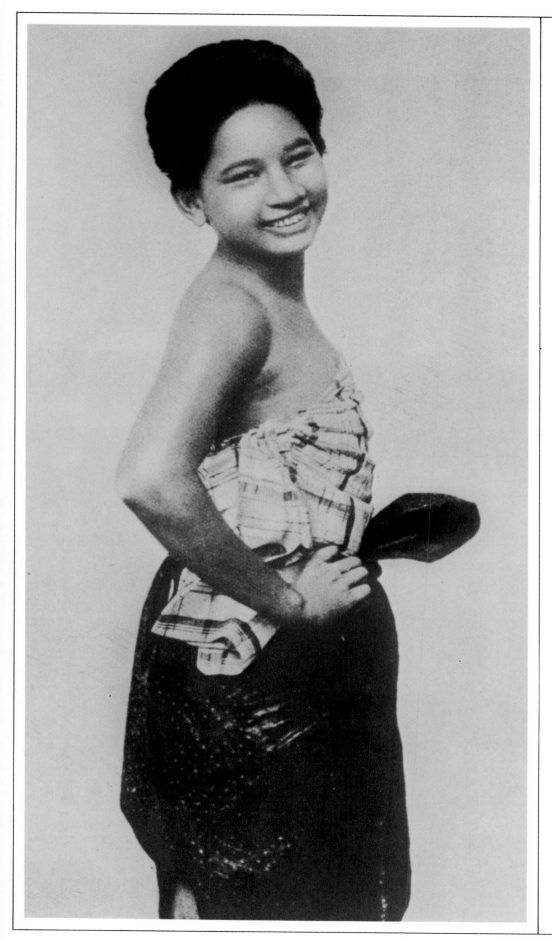

A Bangkok beauty in the casual dress of the 1880s.
(Steve Van Beek)

Bangkok during its annual flooding. This is one of the side lanes off New Road photographed about 1900. Styles of dress have changed but Bangkok's annual flooding continues.
(Therd Suprichakorn)

39

A studio portrait of 1890 with two gentlemen of the day.
(Therd Suprichakorn)

40

A royal barge oarsman photographed in 1910. The barges were used by the monarch during his royal *kathin* at the close of Siam's rainy season, when robes and gifts were taken from the Grand Palace to the monks of the Temple of Dawn. The Royal Barge known as Sri Supannahong requires a crew of fifty-four oarsmen, two steersmen, two officers, one flagman, one rhythm keeper, and one singer who chants to the cadence of the oars.
(Steve Van Beek)

Convicts working at a Bangkok lumber mill, photographed in 1910.
(Steve Van Beek)

41

The grand procession marking the completion of the Phra Buddha Yot Fa Memorial Bridge, centerpiece of the celebrations to mark the 150th anniversary of Bangkok as the nation's capital and of the founding of the Chakri Dynasty. The statue of King Phra Buddha Yot Fa (Rama I) after whom the bridge is named is about to be unveiled at left. April 6, 1932.
(National Archives, Bangkok)

Bangkok's Makasan Railway station on the Eastern line, photographed in 1910. It was only with the construction of the railroad during the reign of King Rama V (1868-1910) that real changes occurred in the country's communication system. The first track covering 71 kilometers between Bangkok and Ayudhya was completed in March 1897.
(Bonnie Davis)

Facing page: An elderly courtier relaxing at home, photographed in 1905.
(Steve Van Beek)

An elaborate ceremony opened the Memorial Bridge joining Bangkok and Thonburi in 1932.
(Steve Van Beek)

46

Soldiers march down Rajdamnern Avenue with Wat Phra Kaew at the end of the street in the background. The Justice Ministry is on the left. Note the Chinese in the crowd with their queues and hats.

(M.C. Piya Rangsit)

A military parade on *Sanam Luang*, also known as Phramane Ground. 1900.

(M.C. Piya Rangsit)

A military parade on *Sanam Luang*, with the magnificent spires of the Temple of the Emerald Buddha in the background. Photographed about 1900.
(M.C. Piya Rangsit)

These photographs of
workers marching near the
Grand Palace were also
taken during the 1908
celebrations marking the
fortieth year in the reign
of King Chulalongkorn.
(M.C. Piya Rangsit)

50

Members of various trades were decked out in the regalia of their occupations. At left are signalmen and ticket collectors, the latter toting first, second and third class tickets to the final destinations of the kingdom's four railway lines at that time, in order right to left: Korat, Petchburi, Phitsanuloke and Patriew (Chachoengsao). (M.C. Piya Rangsit)

Below: members from the Railways workshops. (M.C. Piya Rangsit)

Government workers
marching during
celebrations of King
Chulalongkorn's 40th year
of rule.
(M.C. Piya Rangsit)

Postal workers marching near the Temple of the Emerald Buddha. These are carrying stamps and cancellation rubber stamps.
(M.C. Piya Rangsit)

Bridge builders display their work in miniature as they pass by the crenellated wall of Wat Phra Kaew.
(M.C. Piya Rangsit)

Right: During the celebrations, a grand dragon winds its way through the streets of Bangkok.
(M.C. Piya Rangsit)

Below: Elephants form part of the procession as it passes down New Road in the old section of the city.
(M.C. Piya Rangsit)

54

Part of the spectacular procession in honor of King Chulalongkorn.
(M.C. Piya Rangsit)

King Chulalongkorn being greeted by the foreign community on his arrival at the parade ground. The car is decorated with the royal bird, the Garuda, which transports Rama, the name which the Chakri kings took for themselves. Chulalongkorn was Rama V.
(M.C. Piya Rangsit)

Soldiers and dignitaries
gather at the Royal Plaza
for the unveiling of the
equestrian statue of King
Rama V.
(M.C. Piya Rangsit)

Looking down Rajdamnern Avenue towards Wat Phra Kaew with *Sanam Luang* (Phramane Ground) on the right. Part of the celebration in honor of King Chulalongkorn.
(M.C. Piya Rangsit)

Automobiles were ingeniously and elaborately decorated and formed part of the Rama V procession.
(M.C. Piya Rangsit)

58

Some of the decorated cars that took part in the 1908 parade. The garuda is a symbol of royalty. The center picture shows a car decorated in the theme of the *Ramakien*, the Thai version of the great Hindu epic, *Ramayana*, or "Tale of Rama".
(M.C. Piya Rangsit)

A love of vivid color and elaborate decoration form part of the Thai personality as reflected by these imaginatively decorated automobiles. It is not known when the first motor car appeared in Thailand, but within the first decade of this century the Thai Royal Family and the business executives were regularly using the new "horseless carriages". Two foreign firms were established — Butler and Webster was the agent for the American cars and Barrow Brown for the English cars. Most popular of all for a pleasant, breezy ride about town in the late afternoon was the convertable type known as the coupé.

(M.C. Piya Rangsit)

60

The first car that arrived in Thailand is believed to have been ordered by a private owner, Chao Phya Surasak, a high-ranking officer who was fond of novelty. Putting it into gear and getting it to climb over Bangkok's steep bridges were early obstacles. King Chulalongkorn's first car was a Mercedes Daimler, purchased in France by his son, the Prince of Rajburi. When the car arrived no one knew how to drive it so the Prince himself became his father's chauffeur. The King was very pleased with his first motor car and ordered another one which he named *Kaew Chakrapat*, meaning the "Royal Crystal." He then ordered ten more to give away to members of his family and senior members of the cabinet. Each car that he gave away had a name rhyming with the other.
(M.C. Piya Rangsit)

Seconds after the veil has been dropped from the equestrian statue of King Chulalongkorn (Rama V). The domed Ananda Samakhom that now forms the backdrop for the statue had not been built at the time this photograph was taken. Photographed in 1908 during celebrations held for the fortieth year of King Chulalongkorn's reign. Unfortunately, Chulalongkorn the Great died in 1910, only two years after this emotional outpouring of reverence. His popularity continues to the present day. On each 23rd of October, from dawn well into evening all levels of Thai society pay respect to the equestrian statue of the king at the Throne Hall Square.
(M.C. Piya Rangsit)

Steve Van Beek worked for three years as an agriculture extension volunteer in a small Nepali village before arriving in Thailand where he has lived since 1969. For several years he served as editor of magazines specializing in Thai subjects including "Bangkok Standard", "Impact" and "Living in Thailand". Since 1977, he has been working as a freelance writer and photographer contributing articles to numerous Asian and American magazines as well as reviewing cultural events for the *Bangkok Post*. In 1979 he served as editor and project coordinator of a book, *Thailand into the 80s*, prepared for the Royal Thai Government and distributed globally as Thailand's official handbook. He is also the author of *The Traveler's Complete Guide to Pattaya & Southeastern Thailand*.

Bibliography:

In English:

Graham, W.A. Siam: *A Handbook of practical, commercial and political information*. Alexander Moring, Limited, London. 1912.

La Loubere. *A new Historical Relation of the Kingdom of Siam*. Tho. Horne, London. 1693.

Schouten, Joost. *A Description of the Government, Might, Religion, Customes, Traffick and other remarkable Affairs in the Kingdom of Siam*. Written in the Year 1636. Chalermnit Historical Archives Series, Bangkok. 1969.

Seidenfaden, Major Erik. *Guide to Bangkok*. The Royal State Railway Department, Bangkok. 1927.

The Dynastic Chronicles, Bangkok Era, the First Reign. Chaophraya Thiphakorawong Edition. Translated and edited by Thadeus and Chadin Flood. The Centre for East Asian Cultural Studies, Tokyo. 1978.

In Thai:

Nid H. Shiranan. Past and Present Series. Bangkok Municipality Journal, Bangkok. 1964-65.

Nid H. Shiranan. "Koh Ratanakosin" Tourist Organisation of Thailand Journal, April 1977, Bangkok. pp. 22-25.

Satienkoset, Phankwamlung, Vol. 1. *Suksit Siam*, Bangkok. 1974.

Lt. Col. M.R. Supawat Kasemsri, "Phra Baromaharajawang". Tourist Organisation of Thailand Journal, April 1977. pp. 6-9.

T. Kluaymai na Ayuddhaya, "History of Sanitation in Bangkok", Bangkok Municipality Journal. 1965.

Thepchoo Tapthong, *Krungthep nai Ardeed*. Arksornbandit, Bangkok. 1975.